Bill Clinton
is a real person.
He was born in 1946.
Bill always liked people.
He liked government. Now
he is the forty-second
president of the United States.
This is his story.

TABLE OF CONTENTS

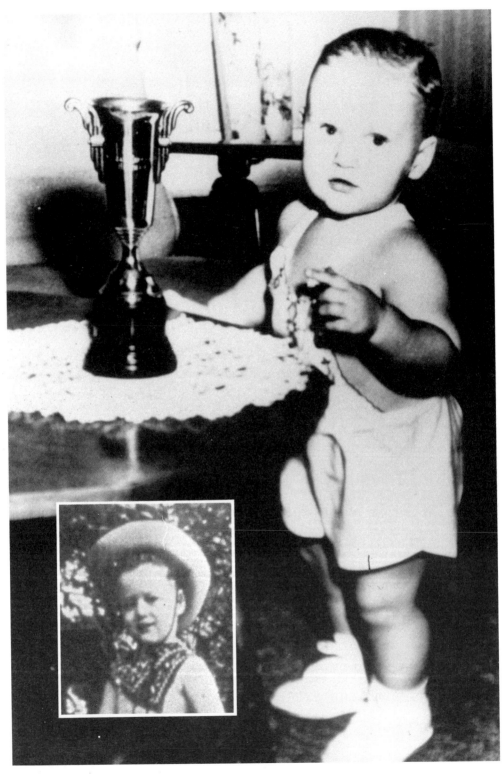

Billy as a toddler in Hope, Arkansas
Inset: Billy in his cowboy hat

A ROOKIE BIOGRAPHY

BILL CLINTON

Forty-second President of the United States

By Carol Greene

CHILDRENS PRESS®
CHICAGO

Bill Clinton became president of the United States in January 1993.

Library of Congress Cataloging-in-Publication Data

Greene, Carol.
    Bill Clinton : 42nd President of the United States / by Carol Greene.
      p.   cm. — (A Rookie biography)
    Includes index.
    ISBN 0-516-04267-X
    1. Clinton, Bill, 1946-   —Juvenile literature. 2. Presidents—United
States—Biography—Juvenile literature. [1. Clinton, Bill, 1946-
2. Presidents.] I. Title. II. Series: Greene, Carol. Rookie biography.
E886.G75   1995
973.929′092—dc20
  [B]   94-36410
                                                CIP
                                                AC

Chapter 1

Billy Blythe

Billy Blythe raced out the door
in his cowboy hat and boots.
He got on his tricycle
and rode off
as fast as he could.
Billy was on the trail again.

Back and forth he rode,
back and forth
in front of the house.
Billy was only four and
that was as far as he could go.

Billy felt great, though,
in his boots and his hat.
All the little boys in
Hope, Arkansas, had them.

But one day Billy's boots
got him in trouble
at Miss Mary's kindergarten.

Right: Billy and a friend stand
with their kindergarten teacher,
Mary Perkins. Below: Billy
Clinton (top row, second from left)
and his first-grade class.

BROOKWOOD

GRADE   I

1952 - 1953

Billy was jumping over a rope
with some other boys.
All at once, his boot heel
caught the rope and he fell.
Then did he scream!

"Sissy!" yelled
the other boys.
But later
they felt bad.
Billy had
broken his leg
in three places.
He had to stay
in the hospital
for a long time.

Billy spent a long
time in the hospital
when he broke his
leg, and still had to
stay in bed when he
returned home.

The house in Hope, Arkansas, where Billy lived with his grandparents.

Billy lived with his grandparents.
His father had died
in a car accident
before Billy was born.
His mother was in New Orleans,
learning to be a nurse.

Billy missed her
and she missed him.
But he loved his grandparents.
They taught him to read and count
when he was only three.

Billy's grandparents ran
a small grocery store.
There Billy met
all kinds of people.
He learned to respect and
care about all of them.

Then Billy's mother married
a man named Roger Clinton.
The family moved to a farm
near Hot Springs, Arkansas.

Billy loved
to wear his
cowboy boots
and hat.

One day a ram butted Billy.
It cut his head and he
had to go to the hospital again.
But he still liked the farm.

Most of all, though,
Billy liked people.
He began to read the newspaper
when he was only six.
He thought about people
and their problems a lot.

Billy liked to talk with
his mother about these things.
She was a good listener.

One Thanksgiving Day, his mother
sent Billy to the store—but
he didn't come home with food.
He came home with another boy!
That boy had only a bag of chips
for his Thanksgiving dinner.

"Mother, we're not going to
hold still for that," said Billy.

"You're right. We're not,"
said his mother.

So the boy had Thanksgiving
dinner with the Clinton family.

Chapter 2

Young Bill Clinton

When Bill was ten,
his mother and stepfather
had a baby—Roger, Jr.
From the outside,
their home looked happy.
But inside it wasn't.

Bill Clinton
with his
mother and
his little
brother Roger.

Bill's stepfather drank too much,
and drinking made him mean.
Sometimes he hit Bill's mother
and little Roger.

One night, when Bill was fourteen,
he took his mother and
little Roger by the hand.
"You will never hit either
of them again," he said
to his stepfather.
And his stepfather never did.

Bill spent hours practicing his tenor saxophone.

In high school,
Bill worked hard.
But he played hard too.
He wasn't good at sports,
but he was very good at music.

Bill won many awards in high school.
At top left he poses with a co-winner of the
Elks Youth Leadership Award. Top right: Bill was a
member of many high school bands. He
also played in a trio with two friends (left).

Bill played tenor saxophone
in many school bands.
He even won first chair
in the All-State First Band.
That was a great honor.

Bill and two friends
formed a trio, too.
They called themselves
The Three Kings.

But most of all, Bill
still cared about people.
He changed his last name
to Clinton to make
his mother and stepfather happy.
He was a good brother to Roger.

In school, Bill worked
with student government.
After school, he and
his mother still talked about
people and their problems.

These five students from Hot Springs High School competed
for the National Merit award. Bill is second from the right.

When Bill was sixteen,
he went to Boys' State.
That was a program
to teach young people
about politics and government.

Bill ran for senator
at Boys' State and won.
That meant he would go
to a meeting of the Boys' Nation
in Washington, D.C.

Bill met President Kennedy in the White House Rose Garden in 1963.

There, in the Rose Garden
at the White House,
young Bill Clinton shook hands
with President John Kennedy.
It was one of the greatest
moments in Bill's life.

From then on, Bill's mother
knew that Bill would go
into politics someday.
Bill knew it too.

Bill also knew that
Georgetown University
in Washington, D.C.,
was the best college for him.

Georgetown University is in Washington, D.C.

So after he graduated third
in his high school class,
off Bill went to Georgetown.

Bill's photo
for his senior year.
The yearbook
listed his many
high school activities.

● CLINTON, William J. — Boys State 2; Boys Nation
2; Junior Class President 2; National Merit Scholarship
Semifinalist 2; Academically Talented Student Award 2;
Beta Club 1,2,3, President 3; Mu Alpha Theta 1,2,3,
Vice-President 2; Junior Classical League 1,2, President
2; Bio Chem Phy 2,3; Key Club 2,3; Student Council
2,3; ARSENIC AND OLD LACE 2; Trojan Band 1,2,3,
Major 3; First Chair All State Band 2.

Above: Bill (at left) was
president of his
freshman class at
Georgetown University.
Left: Bill as a senior
at Georgetown

Chapter 3

Professor Clinton

At Georgetown, Bill studied
international government.
He worked at part-time jobs
to help pay for college.
But he still found time
to care about people.

Bill couldn't talk to his mother
every day about people's problems.
So now he talked to his roommate.
He also was president of his class
for two years in a row.

Every weekend, Bill drove over
two hundred miles to North Carolina.
His stepfather was dying of
cancer in a hospital there.
Bill cared about him too.

In 1968, Martin Luther King
was murdered and riots
broke out all across America.
Whole neighborhoods burned down
in Washington, D.C.

During the 1968 riots in Washington, D.C., many buildings were burned down.

A street in
Oxford, England,
where Bill
studied as a
Rhodes scholar.

Bill loaded his car with food
and took it to homeless people.

Bill did so well at Georgetown
that he won a Rhodes scholarship.
That meant he could study at
Oxford University in England.
Of course, Bill studied politics.

Above: Yale University, where Bill
Clinton studied law
Left: Hillary Rodham Clinton in 1975

Back in the United States,
Bill went to Yale Law School.
There he met Hillary Rodham,
a bright student from Chicago.
Soon they began dating.

After law school, Bill
went back to Arkansas.
He thought he'd be
a lawyer in Hot Springs.
Instead, he began teaching
at the University of Arkansas.

Bill (left) worked to elect George McGovern (center) as president in 1972.

But Bill still thought politics
was the best way to help
people with their problems.
In 1974, he ran for Congress.
He lost—but not by much.

"He will be back. . . ,"
said an Arkansas newspaper.

About that time, Hillary Rodham
came to teach at the university.
A year later, in 1975,
she and Bill were married.

Bill plays with his dog Zeke during his first term as governor of Arkansas.

The newspaper was right
about Bill, too.
In 1976, he ran for
attorney general of Arkansas.
He won.

Now Bill Clinton was on his way.
And he planned to go far.

Bill was thirty-two years old when he became governor of Arkansas.

Chapter 4

Governor Clinton

One day, Bill and a friend
were talking about what
Bill should do next.
Should he try to become
a United States senator
or governor of Arkansas?

"I believe I can do more good
for the people of Arkansas
as governor," Bill said.

In 1978, Bill ran for governor.
He won.
"There is much to be done," he said.
And he tried to do it all.

Bill tried to help schools.
He tried to fix highways.
He was so busy that he didn't
listen to what the people wanted.
So when he ran for governor
again in 1980, Bill lost.

But Bill learned fast.
He drove all over Arkansas.
He told people he was sorry that
he hadn't listened to them.
Hillary made speeches too.
She was a good politician.

In 1982, Bill, Hillary, and
their little girl, Chelsea,
moved back into
the governor's mansion.

Above: Bill was
elected governor
of Arkansas for
the second time
in 1982.
Right: Bill and Hillary
hold their newborn
daughter, Chelsea,
in 1980.

Bill and Chelsea
leave the voting booth
after the governor
cast his vote in
the 1986 election.

In all, Bill was
elected governor
of Arkansas
five times.
He helped
the schools.
He worked
against crime.
He helped
people find jobs.

But on October 3, 1991,
Bill made a big announcement.
He was going to run for
president of the United States.

Just *running* for president
was a huge job.
All across America,
people had to learn
who Bill Clinton was
and what he believed in.

At last, the Democratic Party
chose Bill as its candidate.
But his battle wasn't over.
Now he had to beat the
Republican president, George Bush.

Bill Clinton and Al Gore (left) were nominated for president
and vice president at the Democratic convention in 1992.

During the campaign Bill talked with people all over the United States.
He told them what he wanted for the country.
Below: Bill reading to children at a church in Washington, D.C.

Once again, Bill traveled. He talked with people all across the country. Sometimes he talked so much that he lost his voice. But Bill loved meeting people.

Bill Clinton took the oath of office as president on January 20, 1993.

And on November 3, 1992, the American people chose Bill to be their forty-second president.

The Clinton family waves good-bye as they leave Arkansas for Washington, D.C.

Chapter 5

President Clinton

So Bill and Hillary,
twelve-year-old Chelsea,
and Socks, the family cat,
moved to the White House
in Washington, D.C.

Chelsea Clinton and her
cat Socks watch the
Super Bowl on television at
the White House.

President Clinton signing a bill at the White House.
The new law will make it harder for people to buy guns.

Once again, Bill's mind was full
of plans to help people.
He'd help them get jobs.
He'd fight against crime.
He'd make the United States
a good friend of other countries.

Bill himself had a strong helper,
and everyone knew it.
Right away, he put Hillary
in charge of his health care plan.
Bill wanted *all* Americans
to have good health care.

Hillary Clinton was in charge of the people who worked on President Clinton's health care plan.

President Clinton signing a bill in the Rose Garden (top)
and meeting with African leaders Nelson Mandela and Robert
Muga at the United Nations.

As president,
Bill Clinton
listened to
all kinds
of people.

But Bill didn't forget the
lesson he learned as governor.
He tried to listen to people
and what they wanted.

When he chose people
to help him in government,
Bill remembered
his grandparents' store.
And he chose all kinds of people—
blacks, whites, Asians, and
Latinos, women and men.

43

The President meeting with Japanese prime minister Morihiro Hosokawa (above) and Russian president Boris Yeltsin (below).

Being president isn't easy.
You can't please *all* the voters.
Some are always mad at you.

But Bill Clinton still cares
about people and their problems.
That should help make him
a good president.

Important Dates

1946   August 19—Born in Hope, Arkansas, to Virginia and William Blythe

1960   Took stepfather's last name, Clinton

1963   Shook hands with President John F. Kennedy

1964   Began studies at Georgetown University, Washington, D.C.

1968   Began studies as Rhodes scholar at Oxford University, England

1970   Began studies at Yale Law School, New Haven, Connecticut

1973   Began teaching at University of Arkansas, Fayetteville

1975   Married Hillary Rodham

1976   Became attorney general of Arkansas

1978   Elected governor of Arkansas

1980   Daughter Chelsea born

1982, 1984, 1986, 1990   Reelected governor of Arkansas

1992   Elected forty-second president of the United States

INDEX

Page numbers in boldface type indicate illustrations.

PHOTO CREDITS

ABOUT THE AUTHOR

Carol Greene has degrees in English literature and musicology. She has worked in international exchange programs, as an editor, and as a teacher of writing. She now lives in Webster Groves, Missouri, and writes full-time. She has published more than 100 books, including those in the Childrens Press Rookie Biographies series.

ABOUT THE ILLUSTRATOR

Of Cajun origins, Steven Gaston Dobson was born and raised in New Orleans, Louisiana. He attended art school in the city and worked as a newspaper artist on the *New Orleans Item*. After serving in the Air Force during World War II, he attended the Chicago Academy of Fine Arts in Chicago, Illinois. Before switching to commercial illustration, Mr. Dobson won the Grand Prix in portrait painting from the Palette and Chisel Club. In addition to his commercial work, Steven taught illustration at the Chicago Academy of Fine Arts and night school classes at LaGrange High School. In 1987, he moved to Englewood, Florida, where he says "I am doing something that I have wanted to do all of my 'art life,' painting interesting and historic people."